The
SPANISH-SPEAKING CULTURES
Coloring Book

Anne-Françoise Pattis

PASSPORT BOOKS
a division of *NTC/Contemporary Publishing Company*
Lincolnwood, Illinois USA

To Madeleine Annette — may your
world always be filled with color.

With all our love,
Mom and Dad

Published by Passport Books, a division of NTC/Contemporary Publishing Company.
©1997 by NTC/Contemporary Publishing Company, 4255 West Touhy Avenue,
Lincolnwood (Chicago), Illinois 60646-1975 U.S.A.

8 9 ML 0 9 8 7 6 5 4 3 2

Contenido   Contents

Orientación

La Tierra
en el Espacio

Países hispanos

4

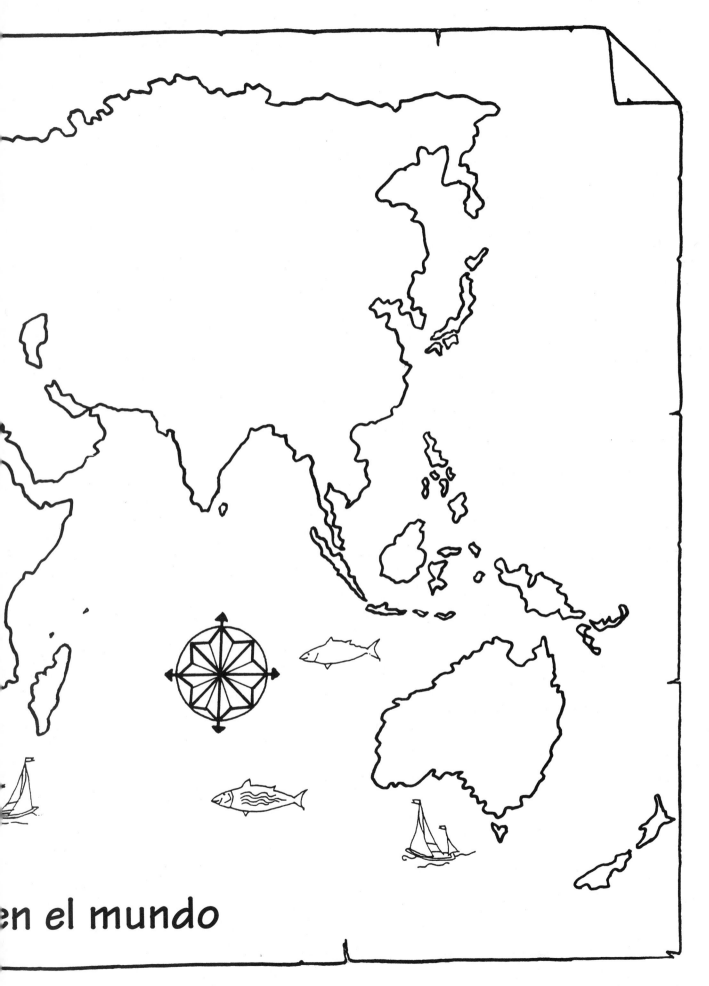

en el mundo

5

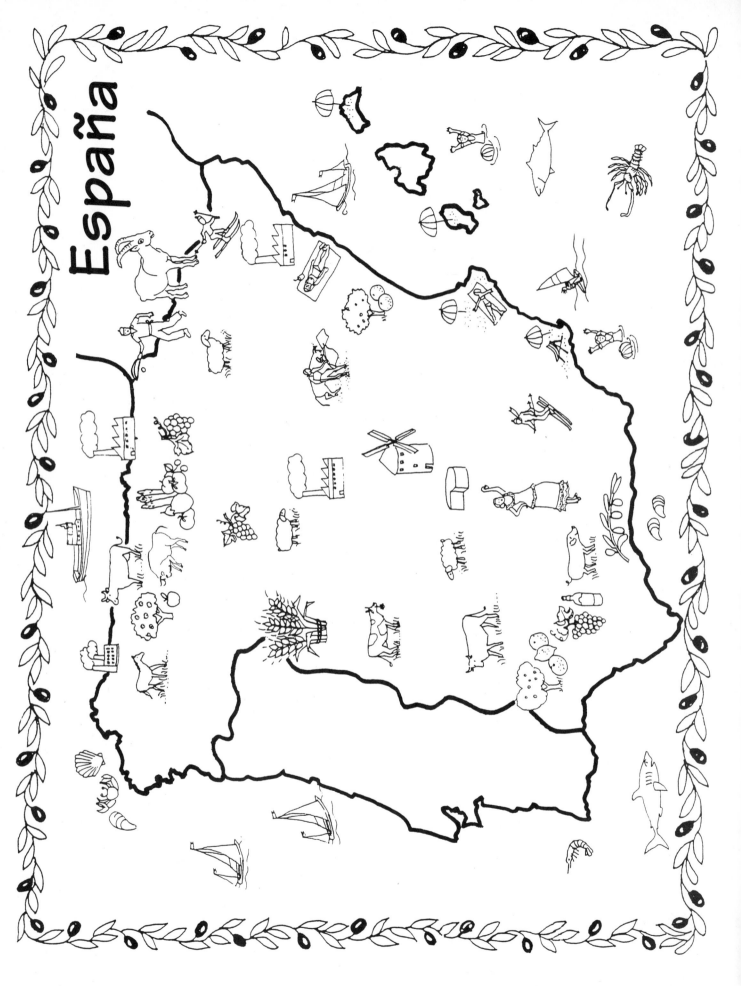

España

6

México

Guatemala

Honduras

El Salvador

Cuba

Nicaragua

La República
Dominicana

Costa Rica

Puerto Rico

Panamá

Centroamérica
y el Caribe

8

Venezuela

Colombia

Ecuador

Perú

Bolivia

Chile

Paraguay

Uruguay

Argentina

Sudamérica

9

Los

hispanos

Los paisajes

Los molinos de viento

Los Andes

Las pampas

El cacao

La llama

El maíz

La orquídea

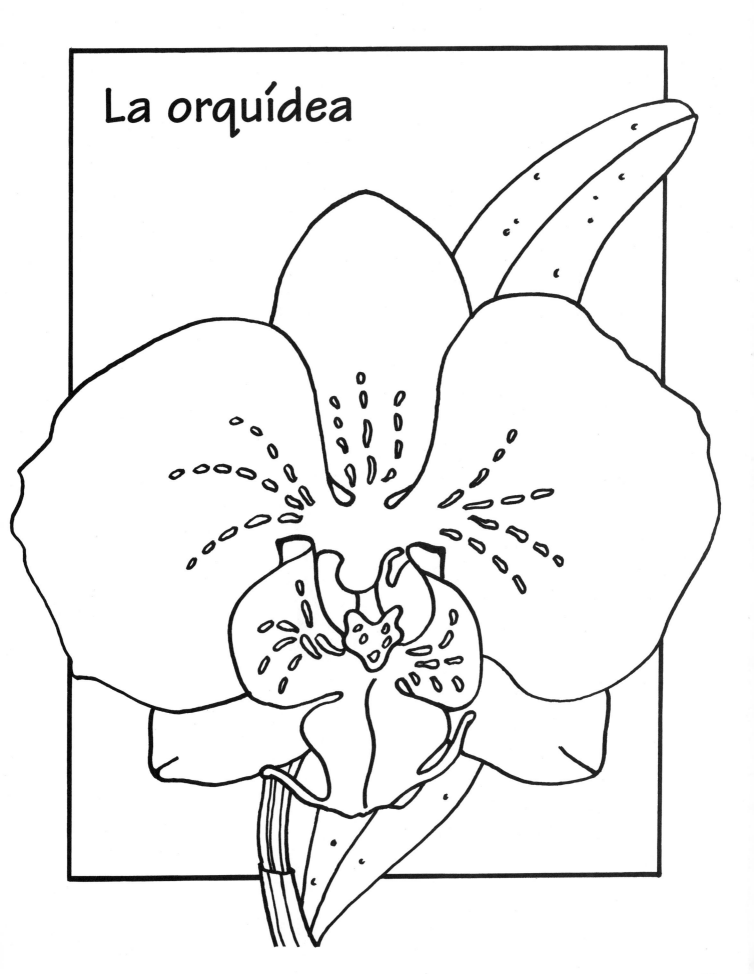

El olivo

La historia

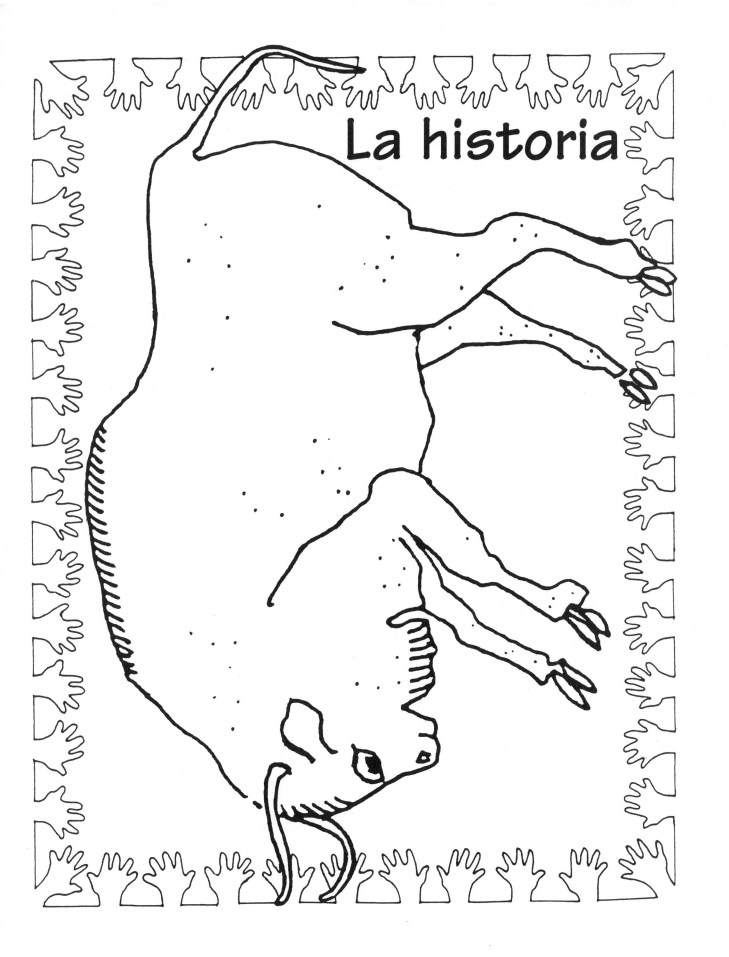

Las cuevas de Altamira

La reina Isabel

Cristóbal Colón

Moctezuma

Simón Bolívar

25

El padre Hidalgo

Los monumentos

Machu Picchu

La pirámide

La Alhambra

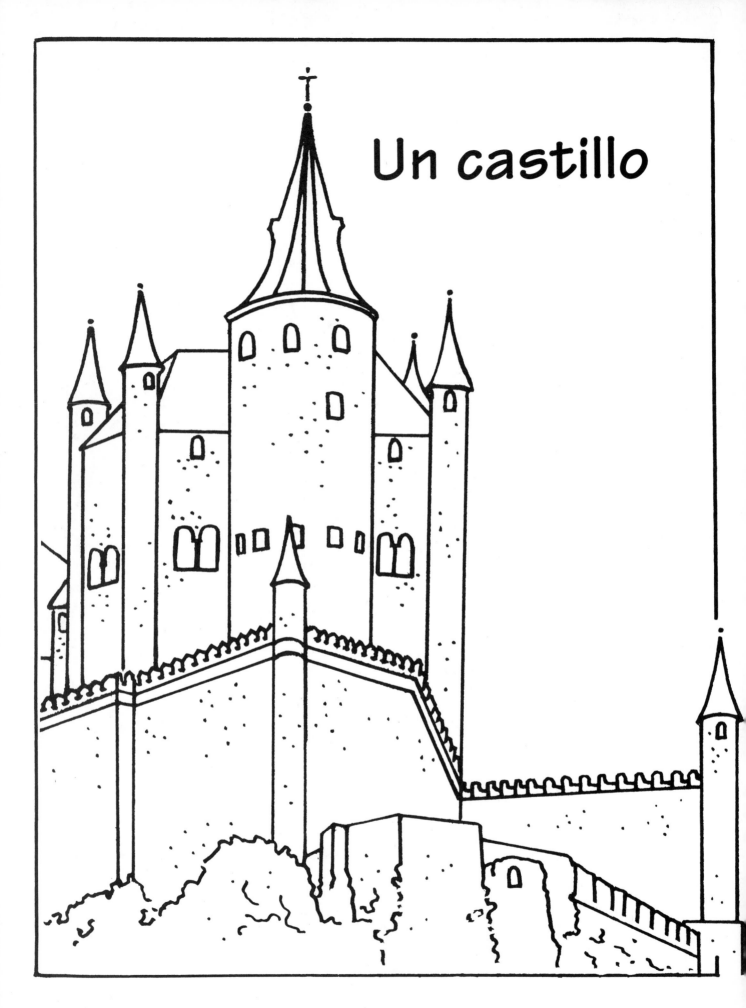

Un castillo

30

De compras

Un mercado peruano

El mercado

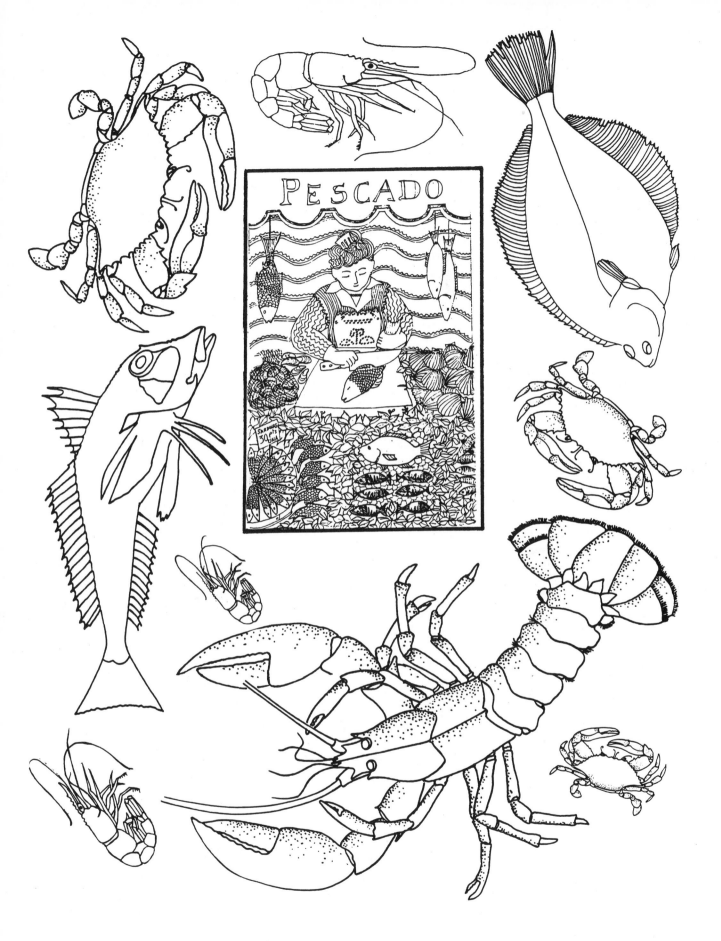

PESCADO

La pescadería

La vendedora de zumos
y aguas frescas

Días de fiesta

El baile flamenco

El día de los muertos

La Navidad en México

Las diversiones

La corrida de toros

El
fútbol

El vendedor de globos

La piñata

Las mañanitas*

Éstas son las mañanitas
  que cantaba el rey David
A las muchachas bonitas
  se les cantaba así:
Despierta, mi bien, despierta,
Mira que ya amaneció;
Los pajaritos cantan,
  la luna ya se metió.

*See translation of song on page 50.

Don Quijote

Artesanía

Un carrito

El arte de tejer

Los instrumentos musicales

Los encajes

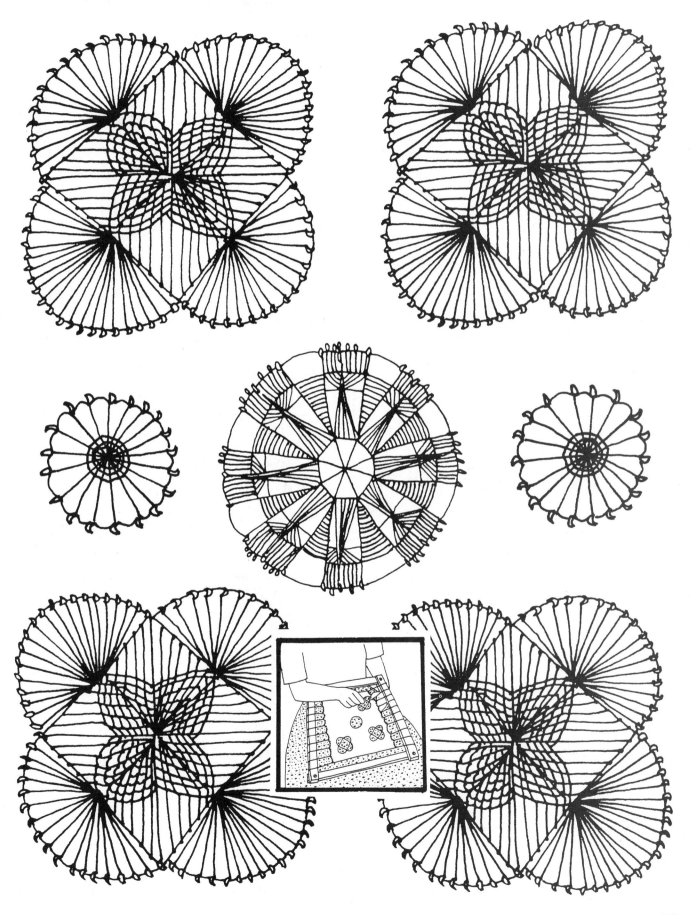

Una mola

La mujer
Cuna

Pronunciation Guide

The following is a translation of the song **"Las mañanitas"** that appears on page 41.

Morning Serenade

This is the morning serenade that King David sang,
To all the nice girls he sang just so:
Wake up, my beloved, wake up,
Look! The sun has risen;
The little birds are singing; the moon has set.

Notes

These notes give you more information about what you see in the pictures you are coloring.
They help you learn many interesting facts about Hispanic countries and cultures.

Orientación   Overview

Países hispanos en el mundo   Spanish-speaking Countries in the World (Pages 4-5)

There are Spanish-speaking countries in just about every part of the world. Why? In 1492 Columbus discovered America for King Ferdinand and Queen Isabella of Spain. Soon others wanted to be **conquistadores** (conquerors) of new lands for Spain. Brave men sailed across the Atlantic to North America, Central and South America. A Spaniard completed the first trip around the world after the captain, Magellan, died in the Philippines. As the Spaniards sailed, they claimed different lands for their country.

España   Spain (Page 6)

Spain has some very beautiful scenery: snow-capped mountains, green valleys, hidden waterfalls, high plains, dense pine forests, orange groves, rolling hills, arid deserts . . . The north is usually cool and rainy in the winter and dry and warm in the summer.

In the South, it can get very hot in the summer — at times, over 120 degrees Fahrenheit! One small town in the southern region of Andalusia is called "the frying pan of Andalusia" — it gets so hot, the townspeople swear you could fry an egg on the sidewalk!

Spain is not a very large country. You can drive from one end to the other in less than a day. The capital of Spain is Madrid.

México   Mexico (Page 7)

Mexico is the only Spanish-speaking country in North America. It has an interesting and ancient history. Many centuries before the Spanish conquistadors arrived, various Indian tribes had built beautiful, complex cities and temples. Two major tribes were the Mayans (who lived mostly in the peninsula of Yucatán) and the Aztecs (who had their capital near Mexico City).

The Mayan cities were mostly deserted by the time the Spaniards arrived in the 1500s. But the Aztec capital, Tenochtitlán, was doing very well. The Spaniards managed to conquer the Aztecs. Some conquistadors stayed on in their new country, marrying native women. Today, many Mexicans are proud of their double heritage.

Mexico is a big country with mountains, deserts, and volcanoes; busy modern cities, sparkling resorts, and remote Indian villages.

 India: 900,000,000   United States of America: 250,000,000   Mexico: 94,000,000    Spain: 40,000,000

Centroamérica y el Caribe   Central America and the Caribbean (Page 8)

Central America contains six Spanish-speaking countries. They are all located within the tropics. The entire region forms an area smaller than the state of Texas!

Despite the tropical location, only the Caribbean coast of Central America has hot, jungle-like weather. The Pacific coast is warm, but dry in the winter. The inland areas are mostly highlands and jagged mountain peaks. There are many volcanoes; some are still active. Guatemala alone has over thirty volcanoes!

There are some Indians living in Central America, but most of the people have a mix of European and Indian ancestors. They are called **mestizos.**

Central America is especially well-known for producing coffee and bananas.

Puerto Rico, referred to as **la isla del encanto** (island of enchantment), has long, white sandy beaches and swaying palm trees. The weather is perfect all year long: about 76 degrees! Puerto Rico is a part of the United States, so the official languages of the island are Spanish and English.

The Dominican Republic makes up about two-thirds of the island of Hispaniola. The other third is Haiti. Many people believe Columbus is buried in the Cathedral of the country's capital, Santo Domingo. The Dominican Republic is home of the **merengue,** a lively dance which features the rhythm of African drums and Spanish **maracas.**

Cuba, the largest island of the Caribbean, actually consists of one large island and more than 1,600 tiny islands surrounding it. When Columbus saw it in 1492, he wrote "It is the most beautiful land ever seen by human eyes." The Cuban people agree — they call their island "The Pearl of the Antilles." Majestic mountains cover about one-fourth of the island, and its coastline is dotted with beautiful sandy beaches and colorful coral reefs.

Sudamérica   South America (Page 9)

South America is a huge and fascinating continent, full of riches not yet fully explored. The continent contains nine Spanish-speaking countries.

Most of South America is covered by mountains and highlands. But there are also jungles, **pampas** (grasslands), and deserts.

The climate changes from hot, steamy, jungle-type weather in the north to freezing temperatures at the southernmost tip.

Some things, such as the climate, are exactly opposite to the way a "northerner" would think. For example, July is the dead of winter, so you can go skiing in Chile or Argentina. However, on January 1, South Americans might go to the beach for New Year's Day — after all, it's around the hottest part of the summer!

Los hispanos   Hispanics (Pages 10-11)

Hispanics are people who speak Spanish as their native language, and whose customs have been influenced by Spain. They are found all over the world. There is a large population of Hispanics in the United States — and they've brought many gifts, such as their foods and music.

Most Hispanics live in the Americas or in Spain, where all these practices came from. After all, when the Spanish conquistadors went to other lands, they brought their language, foods, and customs as well.

These foods and customs were combined with local Indian foods and practices to enrich everyone. For example, the tomato was "discovered" in the Americas by the conquistadors. It was brought back to Spain, and is now an important ingredient in many Spanish dishes.

Los paisajes   Landscapes

Los molinos de viento   Windmills (Page 12)

Windmills are seen in several parts of Spain. They are a popular symbol of the central area of Spain, where they can be seen from many miles away. Most windmills in Spain are the large four-bladed kind.

A windmill uses the force of the wind to do work. In Spain, that energy is used to grind grain and pump water, for example.

Los Andes   The Andes (Page 13)

Lake Titicaca is the highest lake in the world where large ships can sail. It is on the border between Peru and Bolivia.

The lake is 12,500 feet high. Near its shores, shepherds sometimes lead their sheep to graze. The lake is located in the Andes Mountains, an enormous, high mountain range that runs the western length of South America, like its backbone. Some of the highest peaks of the Andes rise more than 21,000 feet.

Las pampas   The Pampas (Pages 14-15)

The pampas are a fertile, treeless area of grasslands that extend for hundreds of miles, mostly in the north central area of Argentina.

You can travel by car, train, or bus due west of Buenos Aires for hours without coming to the end of the pampas. The tall waving grass seems to stretch on forever, interrupted only by fat grazing cattle.

Not so long ago, only **gauchos** (South American cowboys) mastered the pampas and the huge herds of cattle. But now the **gaucho** way of life has mostly disappeared.

El cacao   Cacao Tree   (Page 16)

Cacao beans grow on a tropical tree, which usually produces best in warm lands near the equator, like Mexico and Ecuador.

The cacao was first grown by the Maya and Aztec Indians hundreds of years ago. They used the beans to make chocolate — and as money, too!

The word cacao comes from the Maya Indian words meaning "bitter juice." "Cocoa" is a variation of that spelling.

Today we can thank the Mayas and Aztecs for introducing us to a favorite treat — chocolate!

La llama   Llama   (Page 17)

This unusual-looking animal is a South-American member of the camel family — but without the humps! The llama is a pack animal, used for carrying loads in Peru, Ecuador, and Bolivia.

The llama is a friendly animal, but when it is annoyed, it spits. For example, if it is overtired, or overloaded (with more than one hundred and thirty pounds), it will lie down, hiss, spit and kick, and refuse to move.

Usually, llamas are white — but some are solid black or brown. A few are white with black or brown markings. People in the Andes like to pierce llamas' ears and hang colorful yarn "earrings" from them.

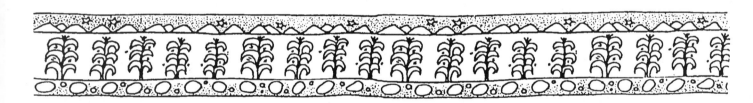

El maíz   Corn   (Page 18)

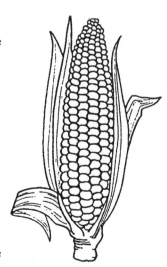

Corn is a very important food in the Americas. It was grown by the native people in the Americas for centuries, and it was considered a sacred crop. There are many Mayan legends about corn. One Mayan legend tells of how people used to be made of maize. In another legend, the Mayan gods hide the spirit of the maize to punish the people.

Corn has many uses in the kitchen. It can be ground into a dough to make pancake-like **tortillas**, a staple food used like bread. The **tortillas** can then be used to make **tacos** and other delicious dishes. **Tortilla** dough is also used to make **tamales**, which are wrapped with dried cornhusks (the outer covering of the corn). **Tortilla** dough is spread on a softened cornhusk and filled with meat or cheese. The **tamal** is then folded over, tied, and steamed.

After eating the corn, people don't throw away the cobs or the husks. Dried corn cobs are burned to make fire for cooking. Dried cornhusks are used to make dolls and figurines for children to play with. These dolls can be very simple. But they can also be very fancy, complete with embroidered dresses and feathered hats!

La orquídea   Orchid (Page 19)

The orchid is the national flower of Venezuela. These plants grow especially well in tropical regions, like Venezuela and Colombia.

Orchids are much loved for their beautiful shapes, colors, and varieties. In fact, there are more than 20,000 kinds of orchids in the world. Some of these plants are tiny — no bigger than your fingernail — while others are vines that can grow to a length of 100 feet!

Did you know that vanilla, which is used to flavor ice cream and candy, comes from certain kinds of orchids? This kind of orchid can be found in Mexico and other tropical countries.

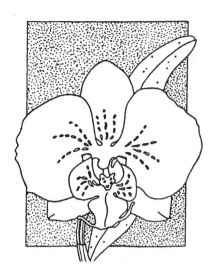

El olivo   Olive Tree (Page 20)

Spain leads the world in producing olives and olive oil. Although olives are much enjoyed for their taste and as a snack, more than 90% of the crop is crushed to make olive oil, which is then sold to countries all over the world.

Olive oil has always been enjoyed for its special taste. Lately, it is appreciated more and more as a good health food.

The olive tree grows from 10-40 feet tall and can live up to 1,500 years! It doesn't produce olives every year. Sometimes farmers have to wait two years for a harvest.

La historia   History

Las cuevas de Altamira   Altamira Caves (Page 21)

In ancient caves in northern Spain, near the town of Altamira, you can find paintings that were drawn by cavemen long, long ago. As you walk through the damp musty caverns, the guide's flashlight suddenly shines on a mighty reddish-brown bison, painted by an unknown hand thousands of years ago!

These caves held their secret until 1875 — that's when a young girl stumbled onto them while chasing after her dog.

La reina Isabel   Queen Isabella (Page 22)

Queen Isabella was one of the greatest rulers of Spain. During her reign in the late 1400s and early 1500s, Columbus was able to sail to America, thanks to her support. She gave him the blessing, money, and ships for his journey to unknown lands across the Atlantic. She and her husband, King Ferdinand, also managed to unite Spain as one country. And they drove out the Moors who had ruled southern Spain for hundreds of years.

Cristóbal Colón   Christopher Columbus (Page 23)

Although Christopher Columbus claimed America for Spain in 1492, he was actually born in Italy! However, he had to travel to Spain for help in his plan to reach "India" across the Atlantic, instead of the Pacific. With the help of Queen Isabella and King Ferdinand of Spain, he made the first voyage to the Americas. After a difficult trip in three small wooden sailing ships (the **Niña**, the **Pinta**, and the **Santa María**), he arrived on the island of San Salvador, in the Bahamas. He called the people he found there Indians, believing he had arrived in India, the land he was really seeking but never reached. However, Columbus made a voyage and a discovery that changed the world.

Moctezuma   Montezuma (Page 24)

Montezuma was the last Aztec emperor of Mexico. In the early 1500s, he ruled over a vast kingdom that extended through Honduras and Nicaragua. He and his people believed a legend about a white god with a beard, who would one day return to rule them. When Cortez, the Spanish conquistador, arrived, Montezuma thought he was the white-bearded god of the legend. Montezuma tried to trick Cortez but became his prisoner instead.

Soon Montezuma was killed. The end of his life marked the end of the Aztec empire.

Simón Bolívar   Simón Bolívar (Page 25)

Simón Bolívar was born in Caracas, Venezuela. At the age of 16 he went to study in Spain. There he fell in love with the daughter of a Spanish nobleman. They married, and he took her home to live in Caracas. Soon she became ill with the terrible yellow fever, and died. He was very sad, and returned to Europe to live. There he met men with ideas of equality for all. This encouraged him to free his own country from Spanish colonial rule. He returned to Caracas, and worked hard for years with his armies to defeat the Spaniards. He and his people ended up liberating, or freeing, six countries in all: Venezuela, Colombia, Ecuador, Peru, Panama, and Bolivia. For that reason, he is known as "the liberator."

El padre Hidalgo   Father Hidalgo (Page 26)

Father Hidalgo was a priest in a small Mexican town called Dolores. He believed that Mexico should be free of Spanish rule. On the night of September 15, 1810, he rang the church bells to call his people to revolt against Spain. Thousands came to fight with him. They fought and freed many cities, traveling almost all the way to Mexico City.

Father Hidalgo was captured and shot to death by the Spaniards. But he is still remembered for his ringing of the church bells on September 15. It is called **El Grito de Dolores** (The Battle Cry of Dolores), and Mexican Independence Day is celebrated the following day, on the sixteenth of September.

Los monumentos Monuments

Machu Picchu Machu Picchu (Page 27)

This ancient fortress city was built by the Incas in south central Peru. It is almost completely hidden on a small high piece of land between two jagged peaks in the Andes Mountains. In fact, the Spanish conquistadors never found it! It wasn't until 1911 that the rest of the world learned about Machu Picchu.

The city and temple are surrounded by gardens, joined by more than three thousand steps.

La pirámide Pyramid (Page 28)

Pyramids are found throughout Mexico and Central America. They have hundreds of narrow steps leading up to the top. The steps were made for feet so small, that only children can climb up easily.

The pyramids were used for many things, such as celebrations or religious worship. They are devoted to different gods, such as the sun god and the rain god.

In the ancient Aztec capital near Mexico City, you can visit two enormous pyramids connected by a long walkway: the Pyramid of the Sun and the Pyramid of the Moon.

La Alhambra The Alhambra (Page 29)

This ancient Moorish palace is one of the great wonders of the world. It is perched on high ground overlooking the small city of Granada, which is bordered on the north by the Sierra Nevada mountains. The palace was built hundreds of years ago by the Moors who then ruled much of Spain.

Although now only a tourist site, the palace and grounds are still enchanting. The palace's walls and ceilings are carved with lace-like patterns. The courtyards are full of murmuring fountains, as are the lush gardens and fruit orchards surrounding the palace.

Un castillo Castle (Page 30)

The **Alcázar** in Segovia is one of many castles that can be found all over Spain. Castles were built for kings, queens, and noblemen hundreds of years ago. Some of the castles are deserted and in ruins. Others have been remodeled and are used as luxurious hotels, called **paradores**.

De compras   Shopping

Un mercado peruano   A Market in Peru (Page 31)

A trip to the market is very important to the people who live in isolated areas high in the mountains. In the big picture, you can see two native women exchange goods as they chat with each other. The market gives them a chance to visit, and to buy things they don't have in their small mountain villages.

El mercado   The Outdoor Market (Page 32)

El mercado is an important place and event in Hispanic life. Farmers come in from the country with carts full of fresh vegetables, fruits, cheese, eggs, and meats. Fishermen near the coast also bring their fresh catch to sell. Artists sell pottery and other crafts. It is a lively scene, and gives people who live in remote areas a chance to visit while they shop.

La pescadería   The Fish Store (Page 33)

Many Hispanic cities and towns are located near the coast. Fresh fish is a popular and important part of the people's daily menus.

There are many delicious kinds of shellfish and fish, and just as many recipes for cooking them.

Some unusual kinds of shellfish — such as barnacles — are an expensive, desired food in Spain.

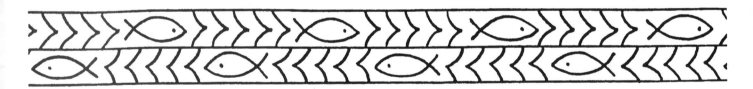

La vendedora de zumos y aguas frescas
Juice and Drink Vendor (Page 34)

People in tropical climates enjoy **zumos**, also called **jugos**, year round. Mangos, guavas, and papayas are used to make rich fruit juices, which people drink in small glasses for breakfast or as a snack. For **agua fresca** (which means "refreshing water"), people add water, sugar, and ice to the fruit juice. **Agua fresca** is a satisfying, nutritious alternative to powdered drink mixes and soda pop. If you travel to a Spanish-speaking country in the Americas, you can see the sparkling barrel-shaped glass containers of **agua fresca**. Slices of citrus fruits, chunks of pineapple, or tiny strawberry seeds floating in the glass jar tell the flavor of the drink.

Días de fiesta   Holidays

El baile flamenco   Flamenco (Page 35)

Flamenco dancing is a special kind of dance created by the people of southern Spain many years ago. It is an intense dance, usually performed by a man and a woman. They clap their hands or click castanets, and stamp their feet, while a guitar player sings a love song.

The woman wears a colorful dress with a long, full, swirling skirt, while the man wears a short jacket and tight pants.

The dance is especially popular during the **Feria** (Festival) of Seville, in April.

El día de los muertos   The Day of the Dead (Page 36)

The Feast of All Souls' Day, November 2, is also known as the Day of the Dead. It is an important holiday in many Hispanic countries, especially Mexico. The Hispanics honor their dead by bringing special foods and flowers to the cemetery where their dead are buried. They feast and pray in their memory.

Candies, cakes, and special items are made in honor of the dead — like the mask you can color in the big picture.

La Navidad en México   Christmas in Mexico (Page 37)

Christmas is an important time in Mexico. Some popular decorations for the home are poinsettias and nativity scenes. Several days before Christmas, many Mexicans begin a special local pilgrimage called **Posadas** (Visits to the Inn). In memory of Joseph and Mary, who could not find room at the inn, families and neighbors call at each other's houses and ask for **posada**, or lodging. They are invited into the home, and given hot chocolate laced with cinnamon, among many other treats. Often a **piñata** is provided for the children, and they take turns trying to hit it.

Las **diversiones**   Amusements

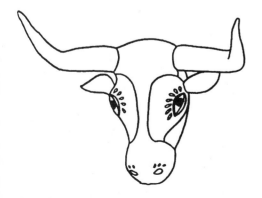

La corrida de toros   Bullfighting (Page 38)

Bullfighting is an exciting spectacle in Spain, Mexico, and Venezuela. In such places it is considered an art, and the **torero** (bullfighter) spends much time carefully preparing himself in the techniques of the fight. **Toreros** wear a special suit called **un traje de luces** (suit of lights) which has thousands of sequins sewn onto the fabric.

Bulls are especially bred for strength and fighting power, and some of the battles between **torero** and bull are frightening.

If a bullfighter has been very good, he is awarded the ears or the tail of the bull!

Bullfights are especially common during town festivals.

El fútbol   Soccer   (Page 39)

Soccer has become a sport played all over the world. But it has always been one of the most important sports in Hispanic countries. Local people are very devoted to their soccer teams and will cheer and discuss them all year long. Young children begin playing soccer at a very early age. A trip to the park almost always guarantees there will be a game of **fútbol** to play or watch.

Just about anyone can play **fútbol** — there is no expensive equipment: just a ball and your own two feet!

El vendedor de globos   Balloon Vendor   (Page 40)

People in Hispanic countries love to go for **paseos,** or walks, through the parks and **plazas** of their town, especially in the evening when the weather is cooler. They usually dress in their nice clothes, and whole families walk together, greeting friends and talking while their children pester them to buy treats.

Many vendors line parkways and avenues, selling ice cream, **churros** (long, skinny pastries), candies, toys, and balloons. Most parents end up buying at least one treat for their children.

La piñata   The Piñata   (Page 41)

The **piñata** is a colorful figure, such as a donkey or a star, made of papier mâché. It is stuffed with candies and other goodies inside, then hung from the ceiling or a tree. Children are blindfolded and take turns hitting the **piñata** with a stick or bat. When it finally breaks, all the children around scramble to gather their goodies.

Piñatas are very popular during birthday parties and festivals.

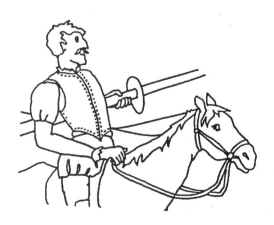

Don Quijote   Don Quixote   (Page 42)

Don Quixote was not a real person; he is an important character in a book. According to the book, Don Quixote was a Spanish nobleman who read a lot of stories about knights in shining armor, and finally decided to go forth and become a knight himself. He had many adventures along the way. In one adventure, he saw a windmill in the distance and thought it was a giant. He rode up and attacked the windmill, got caught on one of the blades, and went around and around and around in the air until he was freed by his servant, Sancho. He still would not believe it was a windmill, and told Sancho that some kind of "enchanter" had changed it from a giant into a windmill.

The book, **Don Quijote de la Mancha,** is still one of the most popular novels of all times, and it was first published in 1605!

Artesanía   Arts and Crafts

Un carrito   Oxcart (Page 43)

The oxcart is a form of traditional art in Costa Rica. It is painted in bright colors, using complicated geometric designs. The patterns for these designs are passed down within families, from one generation to the next.

People don't use oxcarts to get around much anymore. So the people of Costa Rica paint these beautiful designs on their buses!

El arte de tejer   The Art of Weaving (Page 44)

Guatemala is famous for its colorful woven textiles. Items made from these textiles, such as vests, handbags, friendship bracelets, and belts, are popular throughout the world. This woman is shown weaving on the same kind of loom used by her ancestors for hundreds of years. The textile might be dyed by using natural dyes from plants and berries.

La cerámica   Pottery (Page 45)

Water pitchers, jugs, vases, figurines, plates, and cups are just a few examples of the many kinds of pottery you can find in Hispanic countries. The artisan will go to great trouble to make beautiful, colorful designs. Often people will buy a plate or a water pitcher, but will never use it! Instead, they will display it as a beautiful piece of art.

Los instrumentos musicales

Musical Instruments (Page 46)

Music is an important part of Hispanic life. Even in small villages, you will find a local band lending joy and life to parties. Strolling musicians and serenades are common.

One important basic instrument in many countries is the guitar. Look at the other instruments in the big picture. There are castanets, different kinds of drums and flutes, small bells, a tambourine, a violin . . . Some of the flutes and drums come from different South American Indian tribes. They are used to create a special music which is sad yet beautiful.

Los encajes   Lace   (Page 47)

The Spanish conquistadors brought some special things to the people in the Americas. For example, some of the tribes had never seen lace before, and they were fascinated by it. They began to add lace to their native costumes, and then learned to make the lace themselves.

Today, the laces made in Paraguay are well-known, and lace-making is considered a local art.

Una mola   A Mola   (Page 48)

The mola is a piece of art made of layers of different-colored fabrics. Patterns are cut from the fabric on top to show the color of the fabric underneath. Some of the designs are abstract and are based on the patterns of certain kinds of coral. Other molas show figures of birds and other animals.

The designs were originally used to make women's blouses. Now the molas have become popular wall-hangings as well.

La mujer Cuna   A Cuna Woman   (Page 49)

The Cuna Indians are from the central region of Panama and the San Blas Islands off its coast.

Hundreds of years ago, they were an important tribe and had many villages along the coast. Much trade was carried out by canoe. However, when the colonists came, the Cunas' way of life was mostly destroyed. Today, they make their living from farming, fishing, and hunting.

The woman in the big picture is wearing a typical Cuna dress, made of mola designs.

La selva tropical   Tropical rain forest   (inside back cover)

A tropical rain forest is a forest of tall trees, warm temperatures all year long, and plenty of rain. Some parts of the Costa Rican rain forest get more than 200 inches of rain a year! The Amazon rain forest is the largest in the world — it covers about a third of South America.

Squirrel monkeys, parrots, and toucans are just some of the many kinds of animals you can see in a tropical rain forest. How many of these animals can you find in the drawing?